ALSO BY OWEN LEWIS

Marriage Map
best man
Sometimes Full of Daylight
March in San Miguel
New Pictures at an Exhibition

FIELD LIGHT

Summer End—The Dormouse,

Glendale, Massachusetts, 1991-2018

poems and prose by

OWEN LEWIS

2020

DOS MADRES PRESS INC.
P.O. Box 294, Loveland, Ohio 45140
www.dosmadres.com   editor@dosmadres.com

Dos Madres is dedicated to the belief that the small press is essential to the vitality of contemporary literature as a carrier of the new voice, as well as the older, sometimes forgotten voices of the past. And in an ever more virtual world, to the creation of fine books pleasing to the eye and hand.

Dos Madres is named in honor of Vera Murphy and Libbie Hughes, the "Dos Madres" whose contributions have made this press possible.

Dos Madres Press, Inc. is an Ohio Not For Profit Corporation and a 501(c)(3) qualified public charity. Contributions are tax deductible.

Executive Editor: Robert J. Murphy

Illustration & Book Design: Elizabeth H. Murphy
www.illusionstudios.net

Typeset in Garamond & Adobe Song
ISBN 978-1-948017-71-8
Library of Congress Control Number: 2019955236

First Edition
Copyright 2020 Owen Lewis
All rights reserved. No part of this book may be reproduced or transmitted in any form or by any means graphic, electronic or mechanical, including photocopying, recording, taping or by any information storage or retrieval system, without the permission in writing from the publisher.
Published by Dos Madres Press, Inc.

Outside
          outside myself
                    there is a world

—William Carlos Williams, "Sunday in the Park"

for Fran Quinn

CONTENTS

Dusk—a freight train crossing 1
In the bells, ...3
In my N.Y. office—phone's 4
From a corner of the porch a cricket solos 6
Dog days of August, ...7
In rain, I first saw the house, ...9
West Side Highway, river of cars 10
There was emptiness and They, ...11
This New York Jew sits just outside. 13
Not far to the east, ...16
Peggy Cresson showed an anxious look 18
I seem to have taken a wrong turn 22
on the platform, how long. 24
More history dumped. 26
Waiting to meet my roommate 29
Needing company, needing 31
Out of the roadside brush a young woman. 34
Nurse, nurse, I need some assistance. 35
Every country signs the global 37
They come and go, choosing .39
Unplugging Boston's orchestra. 40
un-wanted this yearning 42
She wakes me up (from my 44
another voice 46
one of my patients jumps 47
Where does he belong?. 48
howl. all night howling. 50
I watch the care- 52
order of separation 55
Enough words and their legalities 57

The obvious (not so obvious 58
I always say: cover the weeping bruise,......................60
a view of a field like mine, once crop.........................62
I jumped into the sparkling field..............................64
Rockwell tired of the almost-happy family 66
A fact of history hallows the ground: 68
Facing his own death, a colleague, ...70
Adam does not much like Sunday............................72
Less than two miles from 74
Call me Whitman..82
Riggs: We have only a few mor minutes today 84
asylum words 89
can listen.   Without echo.......................................90
trees planted in the first year, ...92
No footprints, but in the air—sprung 93
Even the common...95
Turning into Dwelling...96
The Right to Know protests the war in Vietnam...........97
On the mall in front of the monument 98
We must not be enemies.......................................100
Not in the hands of boys, but in their eyes 101
the long boat that arrives before living begins 103
the rise behind the sparkle-bush..............................104
The blinking stops...105

Notes 107
The Property Deeds..123
Index of Marriages 124
Acknowledgments 125
Permissions 127

(2018, Glendale Crossing)

Dusk—a freight train crossing
the road, out of the dust back

into dust, once out of the east
and into the west, a long delay

in Worcester, it won't reach
Pittsfield until long after dark

and won't take him where he
needs to go. A lone driver stopped

in his auto. A flickering of metal,
and the low sun behind him

spot-lights the lines car by car—
Providence-Worcester; Boston-Albany;

New York Central; Providence . . .
Against the deepening sky he sees

the horizon hauled by the train,

its pulsing click-clack, rusty wheels,
the strained axles singing of tonnage.

The trainmen know this crossing,
its lights and switches, the couplings

and uncouplings, maze of tracks, maze
of mistakes. Stalled, the flashing arm

before him, he's held up by the train
and held in place, this place, how long

he doesn't know . . . before him
its signaling bells, endless

bells, not chimes not carillons, bells—

(still waiting at the Crossing)

In the bells,
         a black bell
sound, a shovel packing soil
hitting stone and light falls
like gauze once wedding veil.
White churches and pointed
steeples of thudding bells.

The sky drapes too deep
its blue, its unexpected cloth
striping of flag and memory
of anthem . . . my darker light
drops into the Berkshire air.
If painted (by whose hand)?

If sung (what voice sustained)?
A soft breeze hiding in air
shadows across my arm—
asking what, whispering what?
(And I still think about her.)

(1991: State Office of Mental Health down-sizes asylums. Inmates wander off.)

In my N.Y. office—phone's
constant ringing—and my then-
wife's panicked call, *an insane*

playground stampede mothers
crashing strollers, stuffed bears, shoes,
dollies flying—the sandbox—

where the kids play—a man shits
and grunts then paws at it like a cat—
who are these people?—I confess:

I signed the physicians' petition,
lobbied Albany for a plan to free
the state patients with a new

Bill of Rights, an Emancipation
Proclamation. Old guard docs
surrender. I tried to do right,

trying to keep everyone happy,
keeping instead everyone's un-
happiness making me feel criminal—

He rose up, right out of the sand.
Lost a blanket. Nearly lost the kids!
Enough melting pot. We need

to get away. Get. Away.
You need to do something.
Do something. You've got to
*   do something.*

(back home)

From a corner of the porch a cricket solos
   the gaining dusk, a distant chorale

these oboes of summer's end; the August
   heat-hold, the air lays over like muslin

binding breath; these insect-instruments
   unstitch dusk's mauve cover

and through the rent a cooler cirrus stirring,
   a wordless filling, the long benediction

of claret light; by whose offering the starred dipper
   brims and wider yet, the after-glow.

Soft reeds, the chirping slows, the moon's scythe,
   the scalpel cut through darkening air.

(porch photo, The Dormouse)

Dog days of August, the back porch lulls, hours nap-drifting. Dr. Lewis spends the month alone, a sort of sabbatical. He should be used to this un-familied state by now, but he's not. No visitors. Not one. His only companions, an old photograph.

He studies it: just beside his wicker easy-chair, a photograph of a prior owner with her guests. Picture acquired years ago for a touch of local history, now warped by the outdoor humidity. They posed for the photo as a familiar group, on the same back porch. A late summer day, 1922, they sit around a rough farm table:

Peggy Cresson, daughter of
> Daniel Chester French—sculptor of public monuments, of *The Lincoln Memorial, The Minute Man*. She's a sculptor in her own right, sits on her open back porch, called *Il Terrazzo* so named for her wedding last year in Taormina. Her visitors:

Mrs. Hilda Beecher Stowe, granddaughter-in-law of the
> late Harriet Beecher Stowe, and her sister,

Miss Gertrude Robinson Smith. At the end of the small
> table,

William Penn Cresson, much older husband of Peggy.

The photo is attributed to Doctor Walter Lambert, country
> physician. He, too, remains outside of the photo. Had he retired?

They have been here, all along, on this porch, in this house, originally two rooms up, two down, one time a tenant farmer's whose sons found work in a Housatonic paper mill a mile away. Across and down the road, a five minutes' walk, her parents' summer cottage, twenty rooms. This small house renovated for the couple as a wedding gift by a doting father. Father and daughter planned together, and from one letter to the next, "The Dormer House" becomes "The Dormouse."

French replicated his own garden behind her house. His friend, the opinionated Mrs. Wharton, gave her nod of approval after consulting her niece, *the* Beatrix Ferrand. The Stowe and Smith cottages also down the road, past the French's and the curve where the road takes the name The Dugway. The Stowe houses once served as stations of the underground railroad. French later designed their gardens, too—the "stations" obscured. Grandfather Reverend Lyman Beecher's abolitionist debates now part of a dusty history.

He studies the photo, a moment century-old, in the very place he now sits. A town full of history, and he's not part of it. Not even part of his own history. He tries to squeeze into that summer of '22.

(1991)

In rain, I first saw the house,
shingled in Dormouse gray.
Through streaked windows
of wavering glass its fields wild,
impenetrable November
weather raising a dog's musty
history-scent, others' histories,

not a New York smell inside.
(Underfoot, a wall-to-wall patch-
work of multi-colored carpet
remnants covering up
the old chestnut floors,
the toddlers each chose
a carpet square as home-base.)

I heard the agent say—
No ghosts!—but overhead
quick-clicking ceiling feet
scamper the attic, red squirrels
and gray racing the dark.
From the eaves flying-squirrels
jumping into the mist.

(first trip up from New York, 1991, Taconic Parkway,
143 miles to Glendale)

West Side Highway, river of cars follows the Hudson,
we head to the house, station wagon packed three car seats
full across the back three kids strapped in more questions
than cars, crying not crying, give them bottles and sippy cups
Benadryl-laced apple juice. By genie wand—a blue dusk
and almost silence,
     a tape repeating just out of reach   *Beauty and the Beast.*

Our children quiet, our chaos follows—pages of schedules
still turning, meetings, unreturned calls—its own stalking
speedometer. *Tale as old as time/ True as it can be/ Barely even
friends.* My wife, a singer, returning to work from a pregnancy
leave, climbs into the back, into the jumble of child-
scatter.
     Do we have to listen to Disney for this   entire ride?

Two hours and the silver-blue station wagon enters evening
and budding woods and fields gathering along roadway.
Exit to Route 23—*Look at that sign: Hillsdale, 1788*, and
soon, *South Egremont, 1761* . . . silence, but she's not sleeping.
I lost my landmark, sign obscured: *Taghkanik Creek*—native
name less anglicized—
    in tree-top flickers the headlights
       running apace, cross-countering
          the traces of old footpaths . . .

(1992, Glendale, telling a story to the children)

There was emptiness and They,
the Great Makers, dreamed earth.
The emptiness frightened Them,
so They built what they dreamed.
(*No, it's a good dream. Not a movie.*)
From the root of a tree, man
and woman grew tall then kissed

the ground. They fought about
a magic bear tooth. A bad toad
and evil snake also fought for it.
(*Yes, they're both beasts. No beauty.*)
The toad ate the snake and tooth.
Snake bit toad's inside and water
flooded Earth. (*Like when the tub

overflowed.*) And the Makers climbed
a mountain, leading the animals up,
singing a new song and the floods
stopped. The singing got very loud.
(*You can't tell who the Mommy is?
Of course you miss her. She misses you.*)
All climbed onto the turtle's back.

The singing helped the turtle grow
large enough to carry everyone.
(*Can a turtle be a Mommy and Daddy
at the same time? Maybe?*) Singing
helped them grow and that is why

we sing. (*Yes like we sing row-row-row
your boat.*) On earth, (*Yes, there still are

Native Americans, they were born here
 a long time before us.*) All the animals
and all different people found places
to live. (*Like our house here, and yes,
the caretaker, he came by, he's part Native . . .*)
And the earth is always very happy
when there's singing. (*Like Mommy?*)

(photo as Rorschach)

This New York Jew sits just outside
their picture,   (could a Jew fit in . . . here?
Much easier to be a Jew in New York.)

As the Anglicans sip their iced and minted sweet-tea,
1922, already five congregations have formed just ten
miles north, in Pittsfield. 1861, *Ansche Amunim,* Men of
Faith, on Fenn Street—and the first shofar blows over
Berkshire County . . . the War Between the States six
months into its battles with its own trumpeting.

In 1867, also in Pittsfield, Russian immigrants form their
    own congregation.
Am echad. One people. But the Russians congregate
among themselves, as do the Germans, as do the Sephardic
before them.

And in the year of the shared iced tea, Jewish farmers,
eight miles south in Great Barrington, form their own
congregation, *Ahavath Shalom,* Lovers of Peace. Great
Barrington—where Du Bois was born in 1868, attended
the Clinton A. M. E. Zion Church, preachers often
praised the shofar's call of freedom.

Mr. and Mrs. Cresson, Mrs. Beecher-Stowe, Miss Smith,
    Dr. Lambert

            lovers of peace and all humanity. (They believe.)

Now a Jew sits just outside their midst . . . *Hello? Hello!*

>Blast a shofar now to get their attention?!
>*Te-ki-yah-ah. Hel-lo-oh.*

Dr. Lambert would never have acknowledged him then.
A turn of fate, a flip of the calendar years . . . what of
the great Maimonides and others physicians of Sephardic
Spain? . . . and in this present day Lewis had so easily
pursued medicine. He would not have been Dr. Lambert's
colleague in 1922. He'd have been barred from colleges
of medicine in

>Boston or New York
>(whose trains carried everyone to and fro, but not into the
>>inner circles.)

>>Vienna
>(might have given him a chance. Its trains carrying people
>>right through
>>the Ringstrasser into the center.) In

>>Minsk, in Warsaw

>>another great-grandfather—Wolf Yawitz.
>A Yawitz might have been accepted if he applied
>>as Young, or Jung.
>>His Lewis
>>anglicized from Lifshitz.
>The Admissions Committee would still have known.

Resting on his chest rising and falling on his nap's inspiration, respiration,
   Passing Through,

                    another Jew passing through beyond
eye-shot of the photo—Stanley Kunitz.
As if Kunitz this moment sat companionably with him,

on break from his work as a Worcester Gazette journalist interviewing the artist-protestors at the home of the presiding trial judge, *The U.S. v. Sacco and Vanzetti.*

As if Kunitz were a grandfather he never knew, born and raised not far away in Worcester, and in the same 1922

he begins his studies at Harvard. Kunitz is later denied pursuit of a Harvard Ph.D. by Professor John Livingston Lowes, English Department Chair, Coleridge scholar, who tells him: *The Anglo-Saxon students would resent / being taught English by a Jew.*
                    In a murderous time
                            the heart breaks and breaks
                                and lives by breaking.

(Worcester, 1909)

Not far to the east,
from Europe's further east Kunitz's immigrant parents
fled Lithuania's ethnic-lines,
at first count pennies, dimes, eat day-old bread.

A gentle boy sent into public school
with gentiles where a Jew learned to recite
The Lord's Prayer, listen to the King James psalms
become American and Pledge
Allegiance. When the boy was four,

Drs. Freud and Jung train in from Boston
speaking high German, neighbors for a fortnight,
nearby Clark University—*The New Introductory Lectures.*
Do the psychoanalysts conflict in public? *Das theorie's*

pledge of allegiance, dogma's *nein, nein, nein!*
Jung's dreams foretell the future
but Freud searches them like an archaeologist . . .
do tell more . . . Freud angers and disparages
alchemy, Kabala, Tao's all-seeing eye.

Oedipus blinded. Fathers kill sons and vice versa.
In theory and otherwise. Kunitz born half-orphaned
by his father's suicide—drank lye in a public park.
Immigrants have no psychiatrists.

Freud courted Jung, first non-Jewish disciple,
son of a Swiss Reform Pastor. The other disciples
distrust . . .
Freud strolls the garden in a cloud of cigar smoke.
He plucks a daisy . . . *Flowers are restful*

having neither emotions nor conflicts.
His disciples chuckle, following the leader
who will tame the unconscious. Only Jung
hears him mutter: *Wherever I go, a poet's been before.*

Jung (illegitimate grandson of Goethe?) lags behind
gathering the symbols the analysts discard.
In the grass, *Snakes of September* rustle the page.
We are partners in this land,
co-signers of a covenant.

(photo as history, as half-dream)

Peggy Cresson showed an anxious look amidst the visiting group. (Could she have imagined Lewis looking at her many years later?) Her husband, sixteen years senior, was to be going abroad again and would be dead in ten years. She had recently had a stillbirth and they'd have no others.

Lewis, settled into the musty cushions of the wicker couch
                                        half-dreams
Dr. Lambert, locally known for his thespian renditions, asking about the Great War, "And those poems of Wilfred Owen? *At every jolt, the blood / Came gargling from the froth-corrupted lungs.* Is poetry supposed to take me back into the operating room?"

"My good doctor!" Young Peggy reminds, "Are you forgetting your Whitman?—*To sit by the wounded and soothe them, or silently watch the dead.*" The war already old news to her, "All was quite back to normal when we visited," she says, "and Sicily, hardly touched by the ruin . . . Except the ruins." As if the Great War hadn't happened.

"I can't bear another summer without The Symphony," Miss Smith interrupts. The usual: finding a permanent Berkshire home for Boston's symphony. The report: The Mrs. Margaret Vanderbilt and the Miss Mary Aspinwall Tappan have been approached by the Committee for use of their properties. Mrs. Vanderbilt doesn't like the notion of just anyone wandering her grounds. Miss Tappan wonders what would become of her lawns.

Mrs. Beecher-Stowe demurely interrupts her, "Wouldn't it have been better to ask over dinner?"

Miss Smith retorts, "And when was the last time you were invited? Sister dearest, we're B-list . . .

". . . Any news from the judge? What horrible work to be a judge. I almost pity Webster. The trial's over, but his trial will never end. Those artists will be painting it for decades to come. Modern monstrosities. Mark my words! They just haven't left that poor man alone. And I hear Bertha Thayer is close to a breakdown. A persistent young reporter just won't give up, something with a K, not a regular name you'd know how to spell. But at least certain newspapers have been siding with him . . . Peggy dear, just what is your generation saying about it? . . . What? . . . You're not sure they're anarchists? Everyone knows they are . . . that Sacco and Van something, but that would be a Dutch name and I assure you he's not Dutch. Oh dear, we do need the solace of Symphony! Not another summer without."

And just nine years after this back-porch tête-a-tête, Miss Tappan will gift the family's Tanglewood estate. She could not have imagined the children of those shopkeepers overrunning her lawns in pursuit of fine music: Jews and more Jews. Not to mention

Polish millworkers,
Italian gardeners and masons,
the Slovaks.

This group might have envisioned their history conjured
in poetry but not by a Jewish physician; this group who
saw themselves as history: Greeks, Romans, countrymen,
and   their crowd.

       To admire their history, to deny his own?
         A history of coming after,
        with the unwashed in steerage.

If they had received him at all, it would have been
on this porch,

            neither in nor out,
       the breeze off the field stirring.

The best of their generation, trying to be good in their
time. Still, their privilege excluded—

 For poet and psychiatrist, history dreamed in memory.

Passing Through falls to the floor. Lewis startles awake,
picks up *The Berkshire Eagle* with the book. He sits up.
The newspaper is damp and limp, full of old news . . .

He notices a short, inside article. The first issue of the
newspaper was published as a hand-set weekly in 1789,
called then *The Berkshire Star.* Two hundred twenty-eight
years of news. Odd notice amidst all the local ads,
and he remembers . . .

 . . . groceries. Earlier that day he was out. Why bother

cooking? Or eating? What was he thinking? Now another drive back to Great Barrington? To the football-field-size *Price Chopper?* Or the farm stand? Early apples and pears should be in. What else has he forgotten that he needs?

(driving as context, 2018, 1991, 1975, Yale Hill Road)

I seem to have taken a wrong turn . . . ok, no place else I have to be . . . alone in the car . . . passing the secluded property Patty Hearst purchased in the same year we bought ours. And sixteen years before that, in the same week I married,

                                                    a gust
                              tumbles a trash can in the road

she got arrested—

                    like history that won't be thrown out,
                        and my own I'm still cleaning up.

Bank heist by the paramilitary S.L.A.
What made her do it? Loneliness?
Symbionese Liberation Army.

                    Zooming in, what would her grandfather
                            have made of this news?

She's the whole front-page photo—
driven underground, her own infamy,

                          Grandpa's yellowest journalism
                  convicting Sacco and Vanzetti before trial,

long-time fugitive she became
the headline. Helping, was she helping?
She became the criminal.

        Judges differ on her volition
        though all wear black robes.

All have opinions, little proof.

         Not a reluctant participant—
     claims the prosecuting U.S. attorney.

Raped, kidnapped, death-threats
as defense? Her rage,

         Justice and privilege?

her privilege kept her outside of
unprivileged poverty. She wanted in.
Rage not disputable, home front
guerilla warfare, Vietnam's lessons
repurposed
         Have-nots confront haves,

the *haves* joining the *have-nots?*
Time is now to break with inequality,

        acts of emancipation, *symbiosis*

the Berkeley radical manifesto:
dissimilar organisms living in deep and loving harmony, partnership

And after some years of imprisonment she is pardoned
by two presidents. These off-road acres . . .

      These off-road acres . . .
      I understand her need for refuge.

(driving on, he winds up at the local station)

on the platform, how long—
a worry of keeping company
with the book-bound Kunitz,
photo-bound Peggy, newspaper-
bound Patty—him and any one
of them, not friends, tries to

analyze the worry alone,
is alone, watching the approach—
it pulses with light on the iron
tracks a dim rattle, dark vibration
his feet take in, knees sensing
the pitch of metallic keening,

remembering an afternoon's
anticipation, decades ago,
waiting to meet her train—
if there again for a moment
with the train from beyond
Providence, empty, remembering

if he   had stepped ten paces
into the track's throbbing light
to know a version of hereafter.
Soon after, divorce, the slap of,
the wall of air slamming past.
And who might he wait for now?

No one on this train's schedule.
Arrival encumbered. Baggage—
freight, timber, earth, coal, the cattle
cars once sealed.   If I listen
I discern no voices singing within,
wait to know this train's after-haul.

(this train is bound . . . this train)

More history dumped
right in front of me. Here
it's everywhere, can't be avoided.
Good to poke around.

I slow: *W. E. B. Du Bois
Boyhood Home-Site,* a swerve off
Route 23, empty parking lot.
Why have I never visited?

This site, where a family lived
just outside town. How far
do town lines reach? Where
does outside begin, or end?

The site itself seems lonely.
A loud sign, just beyond:
*Respect Your Neighbor, Don't
Veer Off Path.* Anger lingers

but through *the fragrant pines,
the cedar's dusk,* a boulder,
a bench, a marker, no house
or hut at the edge of corn-field

quiet, just after the Civil War,
a town, far north of the line
of separation, safely a century
into land-owning freedom.

Black and White children
play recess tag together, *color
line* quiet enough. But one
child—slight, just one, the *veil*

appears out of nowhere,
it is everywhere, the invisible
divider. Cornfields beyond
the pines rattle in winter.

Town churches send him to Fisk,
to Nashville's first loud lessons
of Jim Crow, the house behind
the curtain of pines, dimming,

and finally *at Harvard, not of it,* 1895,
first doctorate to a person of color
where he's made to repeat his entire
course of undergraduate studies.

Who would've taught *him*
at Fisk, and where did *they* study?
He returned to Great Barrington
to bury a wife, later a son. Where

does he belong? Drawn to the house,
it's gifted to him, never moves back.
A lonely childhood? He dies in Ghana.
Next day King proclaims the dream—

it is 1963, at the Lincoln Memorial,
the Proclamation a century old;
in 1922, at the Memorial's dedication
Du Bois can't forget, "colored" seated

apart, sees the nineteen-foot statue
looming, sees *a temple of compromise*
honoring the union, not emancipation;
can't forget the letter sent him

from a Clark history class—what
teacher allowed it?—*Will you please*
tell us whether or not it is true that Negroes
are not able to cry?   Is it true?

(mind wanders to freshman year, 1969, Ghana to Gullah)

Waiting to meet my roommate.
Orientation. Columbia's ivied dorms.

Guilliard name-tagged to the valise.
He returns late and I'm asleep.

Neither of us act surprised; we are.
We look for the cafeteria, try to walk

in step, share breakfast, reading lists.
What will we do with each other?

> He'll teach me words in Gullah.
> I'll help him with *Moby-Dick*.
>
> Is *Ishmael* really the name?
> Or, *Call Me Ishmael,* just saying,

he, too, a banished son, abandoned
into these academic seas. We'll be friends?

> We anticipate the first exam:
> how are these seas like a desert?
>
> By semester's end we speak
> a few phrases in Gullah, privately,

and passing on campus, perhaps
my seeking too eagerly acceptance

by his friends. Could we all share
language?   Next day he tells me

his brothers told him—better live apart.
He vacates the room. It's empty

and there: *The Souls of Black Folk*.
There: *Fa heal de tree, tek cyear de root.*

(2018)

Needing company, needing
company. All-day *Rising Dale Café*.

Young and old sit around and story
the days of 'nam, days of 'stan, Iraq,

remembering, hoping, waiting
for what? Something to begin—

"Hey Doc, our veteran from the streets
of New York." Arm-punch. Can't forget

how friends are greeted here, forgot
I had an arm. "Got your own Viet-congo-
crazies there too, never been, but wow . . .

God damn that train. Can you hear it?
I live next door. Wakes me up every night!"

Worcester? Boston? Providence sent
them off to Kuwait's oil-fields, now un-
married, unemployed, un-everything'd—

here's to noon's wine, midnight's beer,
in noon haze, moon glaze, jukebox plays:

> *You can get anything you want at Alice's Restaurant.*
> *Walk right in, it's around the back.*

"Hey doc, take a look at those kids nodding out.
Suppose they got reasons. They're not even vets,
hell, lots of ways to lose the American dream.

You think Pittsfield's the only spigot? Black
and White all over the county drinking Kool-Aid,
like he says . . . *you can get anything you want.*"

Walk right in, it's around the back
Just a half a mile from the railroad track

Now all the reports from the home front:
a long table of ex-'s praised, cursed, mine too,

another round rising in the light: *One true love!*

Was everyone divorced, or wanting to be?

Even Stanley's love-knot came untied.
His ex- also made off with a snake.

"Hey doc, hey doc! We should'a listened to Arlo.
God damn us we didn't protest. Go to Canada.

Better country than we got here. And fuck me
who I voted for. Kinda same mistake again.

School yards turning into shooting fields,
home-grown 'nam how're those kids goin'
to learn? No fathers to teach them a trade."

The clock-tower toll, train's whistle again,
signal of transit, of cargo and what is taken

away. *Get on with it.* Arm-punch good-bye.
I feel a rising bruise. Throbbing reminder:

bruise in arm, in body. In mind. *Time to get on!*
But with whom? And what am I waiting for?

(errands)

Out of the roadside brush a young woman
pulling an empty wheelbarrow, shoulders,
arms, glisten against green. In the lane
she stops to pull up a stretchy tube top,
her white breasts rising into the summer air—
he swerves into the ditch, back on the road,
and now from the rear-view mirror—
she's struggling, the top a girdle her breasts
won't cooperate with, resist her yanking,
spring out left and right, she strips off the top,
throws it into her wheelbarrow, struts the road.
Car rounding a curve, the mirror empties.

The house empty, he sits in the drive, the car
a cornucopia of early apples, a last glance up,
in the mirror—and there's—Ursula Andress,
Honey Rider of 1962. There, his childhood
family, the summer drive-in—the cars' pitched,
tinny speakers hung from open windows,
a towering screen, young brothers backseat
in pajamas, a scatter of popcorn, dripping
blue-ice, Honey embraces James Bond in
Dr. No even brighter in the car behind—
the all-night kiss *don't they need to breathe?*
in the night's rear-view mirror looking forward—

and an unfamiliar man glimpsed looking back.

(a dream)

Nurse, nurse, I need some assistance—
the doctor calls out, can't shake me
from peaceful slumber lying on the grass

staring into the mottled moon-rays
in the leaves of the sugar maple.
I've forgotten to go back to work

and that might've been weeks ago
in summer's lost-and-found of time . . .
a burly man with a weedy beard

offers a skein of gauze bandaging.
They bind the patient's head, his ears.
(It's me, now lying on a steel table.)

His ears burst—the doctor explains—
I don't think he could take it all in.
The nurse, his voice not of this century,

contradicts—*My fault entirely. At night,
I whispered words into his ears. Lots of them.*
The doctor clears his phlegmy throat—

*Walt? Walt, that you? God damn! Is that all
that happened?* Bit of glare across the table.
Impossible! Just impossible. Heavens implored.

No, Dr. Williams—the nurse gently
explains—*you were just nine years old
when I died. I've whispered in your ear, too.*

The ghost doctor's seen a ghost—
*All those mornings I thought some whirligig
August-bug was nesting up in the auricles.*

*Just what did you expect him, or me,
or any of us to do with your fine words?*
The nurse smiles; the poet—*Use them!*

(porch as history)

Every country signs the global warming pact, not the U.S. President who's bored by the Earth—temperature rising, turn up the a/c. In Berkshire County, lots of rain, the lawn unusually lush, and the gardens—the dahlias popping, each plant a bouquet.

The caretaker will be coming by—strange man, lives in a bungalow over the hill behind the French estate, slips onto the property fleet as a deer. Part Mahigan, claims descendency from the Presidents Adams. And one day murmuring something about his Auntie Mumbet. All could be true.

Call me Adam—he first introduced himself years ago. He had worked the Dormouse even before Lewis bought the place. Maybe even for the owner before the last.

Adam seems to conjure plants to bloom speaking to the soil itself. He knows more than words convey. The doctor glances at his phone. The calls can wait. His patients often suspect he reads their minds. He is sure the caretaker reads his. Adam calls him medicine man and laughs. He leaves unexpected gifts, today, two books on the garden table, and an unmailed letter that Lewis wrote and Adam found in the field, left on the porch a year or two ago. He's now moved it again for Lewis to notice.

Coyote Medicine by Lewis Mehl-Madrona, lessons of healing from the Native American tradition;

Whereas by a poet he hadn't heard of, Layli Long Soldier,
       a cryptic note on the envelope, inserted on page 49:
       "Read about The Dakota 38. Hanged
       after Executive Review.

       Same week as the Emancipation Proclamation. A
       right to know."

                                         Same emancipation?
                                                     Same week?
                                                  Same *President?*

Progress of emancipation, stalled.
Needed: more proclamation.
Proclaim the question:

if Stockbridge and Glendale were first set aside for the
Mahigan by British colonists rewarding their assistance
against the French, how did this tribe wind up
in Wisconsin, divorced from chartered land?

                                  Promises, promises—
cruel hands that hold us powerless.

            Bare feet, on the cool blue and gray flagstone—
                       even here, the blue and the gray.
                 The stones draw away the summer heat.
The same stones that drew away the summer heat more
                        than one hundred years ago.

(Caretaker speaks)

They come and go, choosing
a spot they believe uncrossed
by snakes and toads. The evening
back-lights the trees golden-green.

If life is long, the flowers, tall.
The owners choose a favorite—
dahlia, zinnia, rose, a whim.
Generations in a single season.

Some can't choose, or won't.
Fallen yellow petals curl.
First frost and the flower-heads
will hang. All lined up.

In their stems, broken necks.
Quickly, quickly, cut them down.
Watching. More to till, to hoe,
now clipping back the dead

branches. Or hacking. Thorns,
nettles, worms and bees. Pricks
of blood drip to ground. Given
even to hungry weeds.

(refuge: Sunday afternoon radio broadcast)

Unplugging Boston's orchestra
from one ear, I hear another
world buzzing with the violins,
cellos and woodwinds, these

insects don't follow the beat,
leading me astray. I am astray.
The Tanglewood concert,
sound-tangle of chorus, Delius's

Sea Drift over the field, its lyrics:
Whitman's *Out of the Cradle*—
timpani or baton-break, tree-fall.
Violins are carved from trees.

O past! O happy life! O songs of joy!
In the air—in the woods over fields,
Loved! Remembering what I don't
want to remember.

But my mate no more, no more with me.
We two together no more . . .
words seeding other words,
and who is to plant them . . . ?

if refused, if refused again . . . ?
dusk's curtain drawing close,
the mockingbird pair, their song
in any voice . . . mocking . . .

Guardian trees
stand the periphery, century-
high pines form the line
of here/there, now/then.

The mockingbirds argue in
old-married-couple squawk-
ing-noise.
        I put the sound-
bud back in my open ear.

(is my ex-'s voice in the Delius chorus?)

un-wanted this yearning
   caught in my memory-touch—
to touch the skin of

  to enter the body of
the voice
         her voice's body

opening like a bellows
  belly diaphragm ribs
and kiss and where inside its first

crescendo
        a circling bird alights
  aloof if hand   if wing
allows a finger's
         feather touch . . .

eluding them   a drifting up to thermal places
   (memory has no rules)
it sensed a migratory flight . . .

(does she remember—I once said
it's here, not elsewhere, why take flight?) the voice
sensing the air's turbulence, found updrafts of exit

left us driving together
   hearing its void, the voiding talk
of children wanes—we watch

a contrail departure across the sky
   a swerving in stilled pursuit
the two of once   *we two, no more*

(silenced: unvoiced: self-analysis of a dream frag-
ment: ex- makes her way in)

She wakes me up from my
dream (in *my* dream) posing as the town crier:
Robert Frost is dead. Frost is dead.

(I for one don't think he's dead.) *Hear-ye!*
Hear-ye means that just moments before
Frost was alive.

All New England mourns. *Hear-ye,*
hear-ye all New England. Same year,
President Kennedy. Country

>bereft, and the Nation's flags
>at half-mast, quarter-mast. No mast.
>No sails to catch the winds, the words . . .

How do I know it's she come door-knocking,
(dead of night? Her voice I'm nearly dead of fright)
tells me I can't have a voice.

I am listening to Frost, not her:
if you'll let a guide direct you
Who only has at heart your getting lost . . .

She says, "Frost would never listen to you.
He only listens to poetry." She says, "To you
Frost means perma-Frost." She says,

"You don't need a voice to admire my *belle canto* . . ."
if it's not 2018, if it's not . . .
the hearth is cold. What kindling? I agitate—

do voices burn? Echoes in smoke:
And if you're lost enough to find yourself . . .
If it's '63, it's twelve years since I was born

and the Worcester Jew (who?) eleven long years
until his first Laureate (he never expects
a poem). *The poem comes as a form of blessing.*

She glares, now opining about words:
vehicles for music, or music, for words.
Whose voice burns?

Even in dream-dark I spy that rolling eye,
an ember in the back of my head.
Just how did *we* meet?

> I dare
> her memory.
> It won't be dared.

(fragments in the clearing, Chris Gilbert, also
from Worcester)

    another voice

in the hearing. Who? (Out of one dream
into the next.) *I wake in dream in the middle of night
and know without looking a frost has come*

    and what, and what?

and is killing the delicate garden plants.
Do I need another poet speaking in my head?
Also a psychologist whom I can speak to.

(another dream, startled awake, 1992)

one of my patients jumps
from a roof, I hear
his pleading, eardrum's
drum-roll, whistle long to
thud, one last, lasting thud—

my children bed-jumping
between dreams, three of them,
like all jumping children, like
my patient jumping, gathering
higher jumps, a minion's *catch-me,*

the pretense of super-man, super-
woman, their mid-air collision's
tooth-knock, they cry like sirens,
and I pretend full wakefulness.
Children crying for their mother:

*Where   is she?—Children,
where is she?*

(The porch at the back of the house, Williamsville Road, village of Glendale in Stockbridge, incorporated in 1784, Massachusetts. Coordinates: 42°17'15"N, 73°19'15"W—a precise location)

Where does he belong?

At the back corner of the house. Porches—where the outside (with its outsiders) is invited in, the insiders may sit near them, protected, nearly in the free air.

He looks out to the field behind the house, similar to the field French viewed from the porch of his studio, just down the road. Similar, too, the field Rockwell liked to visit, just beyond in the other direction. Rockwell came up from New York, stayed, died here. Seems one could make a home anywhere. He pictures Rockwell's work on calendars and note cards. What did *he* accomplish? In town, his portrait faces buy milk and newspapers. One sees them everywhere.

Lewis's field, equidistant between the two, as if the three were one. He imagines continuous fields, how they once were, undivided by ownership. As Adam must see them. Same breeze through the ryegrass. Same angle of dawn and pitch of sunset. What is it about the field light?

Wide, open canvas—

>   A picture of his naked children—
> two, four, and six, painting themselves a chalky gray
>   from pounded rock

     chasing the *au pair* across the field and back
   whooping, thrashing at the air. (Mother's-helper isn't
           helping very much.)

He'd read to them about the Stockbridge Native Mahigan
              or Housatonic.
    The Italian *au pair*, a European invader.

Front-page news, August 9, 2018:
a motorcycle crash on route 7 and a robbery at Nejaime's
liquor store.

Next page: a feature about the high school boosters and
the county rummage sales, and

   President threatens NATO. White supremacists rising.
           Who are the invaders now?

He receives a text reminder: Commission Meeting tomorrow, Rockland State Psychiatric Hospital, 9 a.m. He will have to set out early.

An easier drive than to the city. Mass Turnpike
             to the New
      York State Thruway . . .

(hypnopompic hallucination at dawn, the neighbors' dogs . . .)

howl. all night howling. dark night. the dogs chained to fence-

post lamp-post mail-post they howl, who's the owl, the hawk? hawk-eye, pack of coyotes on the hill? car on New York Thruway, self-driving in the Ouiji-automatic gear, taking the auto westward, Albany, past the turnoff south, can still turn around? spin around? deplorable hitchhiker, dirty sandaled feet, satchel and walking stick. I pick him up. scent of sage. *heading for Worcester?* my ears deceive? kindred-whisper whispering the tune *Pull My Daisy* says he just escaped Rockland State that's me too, escaped escaping. me too a stammer stammering, "I'm with you in Rockland," or out of it. *"Come to my commune if you can tell me when we are? '50's '60's? are you another mind destroyed by madness* heading into the confused sunrise sun-glare *you say you're supposed to be in Worcester you're 90 plus miles west nearing Worcester, New York.* brake-slam! *a short drive to my Cherry Valley Commune come and*

commune!

double-seeing Worcester doubled? it's *my* voice howling he's patting my shoulder. *breathe in deep zen.* your *Worcester, in Mass., 90 miles* east *of Glendale. there're two. give a big hug to Arlo tell him his buddy Allen's listening here and anywhere I think Stanley's fled south to New York. I'm fleeing north. and you? to Stanley? he's everything plus. but in Glendale you're stuck between two Jew poets. Like if Stanley's the doctor-poet I'm the patient-poet. I only* pleaded *insanity man so noodle it out man you gotta choose your own Worcester. You going to be a doctor-poet or a patient-poet? Choose your state. Choose your field. Choose your poet. Better yet be one! Bongo with the beats! '45 Columbia threw me out being homo, "pull my daisy, tip my cup, all my doors are open . . ." add a line! we all wrote it '48, it's late, . . . the channel statics in a dark tunnel. I make out his voice-echo echoing you know knowing Dr. Williams? William? hates Pound's anti-semitic poundage. Williams delivered me delivering into this world a poet man he's it! good start for a poet . . . and who, who will deliver you*

            youou   YOUOUUUUU

howling all night. dark light lightening. dogs, dogs're chained.

(2018, foggy morning memory, 1967, high school
health class)

I watch the care-
taker from the window
dead-heading dahlias.

Caretaking, caregiving,
from the window
watching color, the many

roses clipped, blooms
drop. What some think
original sin, I diagnose

original wound. A garden
of beauty, not sustenance.
What sustains—

Mr. Clay asks our sophomore
class—*what is health? And what
is cure?* He tosses

a three-inch health text
and lesson plans into the trash.
Disease as an experience

*of the mortal mind; it is fear
made manifest in the body.
And the spirochetes of v/d?*

(Jocks pounding their desks.)
The teacher prayed
for his body's own healing,

and the basal cell
stigmata on the back
of his hand crawled

out from under
the bandage, defying
all boundary of

bandage, defying prayer.
How long had he kept it
secret? It swam his blood

into his lungs, fought
his breath, ate it,
the very air of breath

and prayer itself. Disease
ridding the self of self,
a growing self-malignancy,

whole albums of selfies,
pages and more of selves
posing for posing self.

The mirror is not enough.
Adam says: *first heal the root.*
From the window I watch

his toil, flower-heads
fall aground, around.
A sprig of rosemary, a shake

of saved seeds, he sets small
fires. By morning, turns ash
into the root's damp soil

gardening as his namesake
long ago conceived:
to till and to tend. How then

do I call this garden mine?
A plot of land, a plot
of history. By whose hand?

                                And when?

(August, 2011)

      order of separation
orders of magnitude of separations

a railroading cross-examination in the sweltering courtroom

when you . . . ?   were you . . . ?   if you . . . ?

vagus nerve buzzes with electrons a galloping heart uncalmed
drives the gut, gut twisting, all thirty feet in turmoil,

why is she smiling? Lawyers marshal me out of view, advise
to avert eye-contact five-year flashback: Dr. Lewis's self-diagnosis:

Courtroom PTSD, in public, a pilloried sinner . . . (I flee to the house
in Massachusetts, a great tradition of marital bliss there—

Hawthorne retreats, a cottage on Stockbridge Bowl, writes
"Tanglewood Tales," *a peculiar, quiet charm these broad meadows*

better than mountains, they do not stamp, stereotype themselves
into the brain, and grow wearisome . . . I return to court next day)

a patient sits a few bench-rows back, waiting his turn to argue
alimony. Sinners, winners, losers in the daily marriage trials.

She'll get the city apartment. Am I getting gypped with left-overs,
a run-down Dormouse? *Charm of broad meadows?* I need it?

Dr. Williams, physician-poet (how did he doctor and write?):
Divorce is
the sign of knowledge in our time,
divorce! divorce!

In America, one divorce approximately every 36 seconds.
Nearly 2,400 divorces / day, 16,800 / week, 876,000 / year.

In New York, "no-fault" divorce. I do, I do, now and forever absolve her not. Vows and ows. A manic raven. Nevermore.

(the underground)

Enough words and their legalities—
I check the cellar foundation.
Clerestory pane knocked out. Night wind
knocking in. Stones separating. Wood-
creak, scattering mice, their droppings,
and basement whirls of dust-noise.

Skeletal pilings shoulder the cross-
beams hold up the floors overhead.
From under the furnace, I hear
a lone cricket, a weakened chirp
begging for more heat, a sputtering,
burning in this furnace childhood fear,

its insulated arms stretch along the ceiling,
linger in the dark, reach up into the house.

(2018)

The obvious (not so obvious
in the midst of). The day

full of drifting mist (overcast).
I'm drawn to the field again,

the day before, or after.
(A day's time before and after.)

Deer trail crossing the far end.
Scatter of wild turkey feathers.

(Nightly passage. A rushed flight.)
As if the sudden flapping lingers
in the stealth of a coyote ambush.

Almost extinct, a dozen-fold flock
hovers just at the field-edge.
Has Adam summoned them?

At wood-edge, an old pine,
a trunk-long lightning rip
still open, still bleeding sap.

(From a storm decades ago.)
I touch the tree-wound.
(And my storm, this decade.)

On my fingers the scent, the stickiness
carries forward. *No-see-ums* buzzing
about my head, (ears) and eyes.

What do those little gnats see
in *my* eyes?   The limits,

the craning stretch of a personal life—
*see more—look—*buzzing*—looking*

further afield, more light than a pair
of human eyes can see, they lend

their thousand prismatic orbits.

(2018, 1781)

I always say: cover the weeping bruise,
   apply ointment and a bandage.

Adam says: *show the bruise,*
   to air and sun and rain,

air's the best salve. Adam says:
   show the wound. Let it tell.

Words in the air bring light.
   Words in the air bring freedom

to bruise and wound
   to break and burn,
                  eyes burn red

and breath-gasp the mangle of injury,
   if wind can carry word . . .

Which wounds to cover, which expose?
   The wound became the hero:

(long ago his Auntie Mumbet, step-great-great-grandmother of Du Bois,

     born into slavery, 1744, in Claverack, New York, Pieter Hogeboom's farm, at age seven, "given" to his daughter Hannah on her marriage to John Ashley and was moved to Sheffield, Massachusetts. She

married, had a child, Little Bet. Her husband did not
return from the Revolutionary War. Vile-tempered
Mistress Hannah one day aimed to strike Little Bet with
a hot shovel. Mumbet interposed, took the shovel-blow
to her arm. All winter, the wound festered and oozed
and she refused to cover it up. Asked what had happened
she'd reply—*Ask Missus*. She heard the newly ratified state
constitution read in public in the Sheffield Commons,
insisted—

>   *I ain't no dumb critter, won't the law give me freedom?*—

found her way to a young lawyer, Theodore Sedgwick in
nearby Stockbridge. With another slave of the Ashleys,
Sedgwick argued her case for freedom. *Brom and Bett
v. Ashley* heard before the County Court of Common
Pleas in Great Barrington in August, 1781. The jury
ruled in Bett's favor. And after, slavery banned in the
Commonwealth of Massachusetts, her freedom . . .

(from French's summer studio, 2018, 1929)

a view of a field like mine, once crop
now vista, French walked the studio porch.
How much of its light could his mind hold?

He carried the light of these acres with him.
Sculpting his Lincoln, each day he'd wheel
the model out the studio's side, outside.

Even now, he wanted to see his Lincoln
outdoors again, couldn't let the statue rest.
Shadows worked like another set of hands

changing the face. Who is this Lincoln?
The dedication, already seven years ago.
He remembered sketching, sculpting,

re-sculpting. His hands were thinking.
To hammer emancipation into stone,
to etch light into the nation's memory

and future. Lincoln's right hand is open,
the left, clenched; a foot ready to stride forward,
one hesitant in the next step he will take.

Light from his marble eyes filled the studio.
Where would it carry his words and deeds?
The sculpture often hovered above itself.

He knew the marble's flaws—but the man's?
Back in the studio, in the waning light,
he regarded another which would be his last

rendering—Andromeda—stone smooth
as skin. Was it love chained to a craggy rock?
Or the guilty myth of a parent's error

bound into his child?   He watched Peggy
watching the nation honor him. Her sculpting?
Many successes but   Andromeda's chains

were thick and heavy.   I imagine his nightmare:
a vandal chisels through the chains that hold her.
She disappears into the sky of many stars—

(my elder daughter, during the divorce, 2011,
recalls arriving late one June night, 1992, to The
Dormouse)

I jumped into the sparkling field my baby sister crying
the whole long way she broke my ears
I ran from the car
the field filled with sparkling light
the night and bits of light across the lawn
and in the trees in blinking air
you said they're fireflies I said they're stars
they're falling stars we're rich with gold
I tried to fill my pockets for us both
with flying bits of flying gold—

> You pointed higher and higher, said
> *there, there are two bears, the mother Ursa Major*
> *and her baby Ursa Minor following behind—*

whose footsteps I now heard a thump
another thumping behind
you tried to catch me
and shadows followed growing tall
a thumping paw
I heard them growl who picked me up I cried
I cried—*The bears! The baby's crying, she's crying.*
I'm afraid of the mother—

and yes, I, your daughter, knew bears don't cry.
I had heard the baby from the pink crying room.
I was crying our house seemed miles away and—

Please, lock the doors! Thieves!—Remember?
You knew they were dippers, the Big and the Little,
and you called them bears. Bears!
I couldn't know constellations don't fall.
And why bring home a constellation of children
just what did you imagine you said
you wouldn't
answer   with dippers we'd have sipped
              long sips from that sky together.

(1964, a nearby field, he recalls another neighbor)

Rockwell tired of the almost-happy family at Thanksgiving. Every face has another story, even a face shown in town— *The Gossips, The Runaway, Game of Marbles.* Never intended them for calendars. Afternoons, he'd bike past the Sedgwick house, down Main Street,

past Riggs's Hospital, to an estate's field overlooking the psychiatric hospital. He came here to rest his eyes. He moved to Stockbridge for the hospital, to get help for his wife, Mary. Five long years gone, at night he still felt her darkness. Her unresolving depression

changed him, too. Made him think about people—all people—in a different way. Rich, poor, black, white—what surprises await coming *Home for Christmas* . . . He'd never shake Mary's sadness. He liked this field, with just a road between, lying almost continuous to

Chesterwood and the studio where Mr. French re-created the great emancipator. He feels a kinship, the sculptor he never knew. Rockwell once painted a young Lincoln arguing an impossible case, *Lincoln for the Defense.* French's Lincoln, poised at the unfinished task.

The country, not yet emancipated. Maybe never would be. A hundred years later, then add a hundred. *Where will we be?* If only his illustrations did the world-work that French's statue does. Thousands a day view him,
and what do they see? The problem, still here:

The Problem We All Live With, in *Look* magazine, the centerfold, 1964—

and look between the marshals, a small girl, eyes forward,
not looking—

"Nigger" graffitied on the wall—

six-year-old Ruby Bridges, white jumper, bow-tied behind,
notebook, pencil, ruler in hand, marched to school,
William Frantz Elementary. Marshals without faces, in
other paintings
friends and acquaintances stand as models. Rockwell
paints witnesses from town—

1964 town census 2,161—
    Look's readership 53 million—
        U.S. population 192 million—

shopkeepers and teachers, barber and policeman, firemen
and country doc. He knew these folks, knew they wanted
everyone to have a fair shake. Some saying his illustrations
are too popular. So be it! Let the whole town speak,
looking out to the nation, speaking.

(Great Barrington Town Hall, c.1874, built near
the 1764 court house.)

A fact of history hallows the ground:
the miraculous—Mumbet's trial,
that justice was, could be, will be done?

Happening almost a century before
Lincoln's Emancipation Proclamation,
and his order of decimation—

that word—*To kill one in ten*
as punishment for the whole group.
"Civilizing" Romans invented

the ploy, the Nazis' inspiration.
One becomes nine. Disposed of.
Der Judenrein, cities cleansed of.

One left to become the seed?
So few Jews left. Become a Jew?
Become the Other. Become

the other's decimation.
The generals first demand all
one thousand of the Dakota

"insurgents" be hanged.
Almost 380 brought to trial.
Fast evidence, fast testimony,

Lincoln, Commander-in-Chief,
tries to placate, not suffocate,
to moderate, not decimate.

Killing Dakota to save Dakota?
Same week U.S. slavery becomes
illegal. Question the Dakota 38:

the question defies justice.
Miraculous, Mumbet's 1781 trial.
Question: does Democracy survive?

(nearby, Fairview Hospital, also Great Barrington)

Facing his own death, a colleague,
a young hospital resident, writes—

If you ask—why me?—
ask instead—why not me?

Bibles of betrayal. And rage
abrupt as summer weather.

As if the view were fair,
the sky clears. (What blue?)

The problem is collective,
what all come to live with,

and he came to the moment
when breath becomes air, when both

breath and air grow taller yet,
hover as created, find their first,

their last moments, if indecision,
(a pause, moving into, or out of,

the *if,* what *if* that shade of blue
is the fact of an other-worldly hue?)

Not time at the end. Not time
to understand the given time.

Confusions of rage (and weather),
what can be healed, and what

can never be. Within love,
other love. A man is never

who he starts out to be . . .
                nor is a country . . .

(Adam's complaint)

Adam does not much like Sunday-
Bible stories and sermons,
that Go-Down-Moses hymn,
the bulrush basket floating along
the Housatonic; or that Onward-
Christian-Soldiers hymn U.S. Presidents
all sing that makes him shudder.

In the forest, he can see old Noah
walking the woodland paths calling
the birds, bear, the great pond turtle,
the toad that swallowed the snake and tooth
and the flood gushes into the valley,
and covers the mountain, he hears
the Creator speaking through clouds

*Noah, Noah—Shape for me now
a great long boat. By word, in seven days,
I will unmake the world.* Adam sees
the great rainbow streaming the sky
from the great Creator's single eye,
a bridge arcing the great boat's bow,
the evening dove that does not return.

For all this—the Creator will not merit
Noah among the great first fathers.
Sunday-Bibles call him righteous—
but *just for his time*?! Maddens Adam.
His grievous wrong-doing? He planted
the first vineyard, drank the first wine.
No one warned him he'd get drunk.

Injustice written into the Bible,
who needs it? The new testament
wants him baptized! The white, hairy-
mouthed god blames Noah with praise
stuck in his throat like a fish bone. Stuck
in Adam's head a portrait of this god
as a high-collared U.S. President . . .

He can hear animals stirring in their sleep . . .
From the forest, the field light shimmers.

(Lewis walks into town)

Less than two miles from the Dormouse, Lewis comes to the psychiatric hospital, itself like a gilded-age "cottage," right on Main Street. A former student, now the hospital's director, has asked him to consult on a troubling case, an "old-fashioned" psychotic. He'd like a break from such work, obliges, but fears he's left his doctor's mind on the back porch,

thinking of Mrs. Mary French, Mrs. Peggy Cresson, and Mrs. Mary Rockwell, all who "visited" the hospital: Mrs. French for insomnia and neurasthenia; Mrs. Rockwell, depression; Peggy Cresson, rumored to have once checked herself in. Norman Rockwell himself consulted at Riggs to help ease the toll of his wife's illness.

Lewis remembers back to the backward state hospital he would visit as a student. The language itself dazzled. He'd linger with the words forgetting to ask more about the person or make sense of the story. Clang Associations: *bell, well, sell me the devil's hell*; Word Salad: like pages of the dictionary tossed into the air—*the dahlia's turtle, the train's porch*; Idea of Reference, when a tree spoke personally across the field—*you have been chosen for a life of meritorious words, yes you!*—

   images of Illusion,
   fantasies of Delusion,
   ghosts of Hallucination—

he'd sit mesmerized by the endless flow of words.

It seems to him that he must now be missing his regular office hours. Or missing his patients. He had wanted to get away from the hospital, yet here he is, drawn back, as if another self were greeting him. To the swirl of unchallenged words . . .

Colleague: So good of you to interrupt your down-time . . . (rushing) . . . she calls herself *Betty the Lesser Vanderbilt*. She's been here three months. None of the usual antipsychotics seem to touch her. Her mood's mostly chipper, and she seems to enjoy her stay. She only becomes morose when we talk of discharge to a supervised residence—Gould Farm would serve her well. There's a family trust which she can access for health and welfare, but we'd like to move her.

Family: her grandmother spent time at Chestnut Lodge, and her mother seems to have suicided when the child was six. She carries a Mammie-doll everywhere. Says it's all she has from her mother. Lately she's been talking about wanting to become a Jew and obsessing about Peggy Cresson. She had worked as a librarian somewhere, maybe even locally. It's perplexing. You always taught us, there's truth in delusion. Then I remembered you live up by Chesterwood where that Cresson woman lived. You might help us unravel her delusion. What's true in this time-warp . . . ?

Formulation: a middle-aged woman, feels herself on the fringe of an imagined society, early maternal loss, intractable manic-depressive illness, possibly schizo-affective. We're eager for your thoughts . . .

So here we are and here's Miss Betty, and Betty, here's Dr. . . .

Betty: Dr. Riggs, I do thank you.

Colleague: (interrupting her) No Betty, this is Dr. Lewis. A psychiatrist from New York. A Jewish psychiatrist. You've been talking about Jews… (Lewis motions her to go on.) I've got to go but I'll be back shortly.

Betty: But Riggs, I did overhear you talking about Will and Agnes Gould again. Noble their undertaking, those Goulds, but their crazy farm is not for me. Well-intentioned people, but Aunt Emily, that is, Emily Thorn Vanderbilt, and cousin Emily Vanderbilt Sloan just won't hear of it. I know they want me back at Elm Court. I think, dear Riggs, you sometimes forget who I am, though of course, we are more interested in who I might become. Isn't that right, Riggs? You remember, I started the summer off with other cousins in Oyster Bay. Every night I'd pace holding my head saying *Oy, oy, oy,* which

	they didn't like, and is why they shipped me off to Elm Court—with its one hundred and six rooms, I had a third-floor back room, there's enough hallway for a chronic insomniac like myself . . ."
Lewis:	Miss Vanderbilt, remember I'm Dr. Lewis . . .
Betty:	Come now, Austen. Out with it—you thought me a bearcat at Frelinghuysen's party a few weeks back when I asked you to dance. Was it all that jizz in their jazz? Was it Jack Teagarden or Jelly-Roll Morton? I'd have thought myself a sweet Sheba, no? A real "Dark Eyes." Anyway, listen up, sweetie, at thirty seven, I have no prospects for marriage, and I'm an embarrassment to the family. Quite frankly, I suspect they want to divorce me. Friends are no better and . . .
Lewis:	Tell me about your friends. I understand you count Peggy Cresson among them? Is that so?
Betty:	Come now, Riggs, you don't have to say, but you know that I know that you know. Now I hardly think of her as a friend. She hasn't been to visit. And you know that I know that she was, shall we say, quite comfortable here. I'm none too pleased with her. Non-plussed, would be the word. And I'm non-pussed, too, but that's something else entirely. Ever

	since she married in Italy. She didn't invite me and we'd been friends since our days at the Berkshire School . . . or was it the Brearley School. I should remember better, about herself and myself . . . oh yes, her beau was killed in the Great War . . . isn't that right, Riggs?
Lewis:	Betty, I don't know.
Betty:	I'm quite certain I saw a photo of her taken at a patient dress-up party. I am right, Riggs, am I right? And you, you let a patient dress-up in Ku Klux Klan robes, and another with blackface. I'm right, Riggs? Is that what you're hiding?
Lewis:	Even if I were Dr. Riggs, I couldn't speak about another patient.
Betty:	How convenient. Hide behind privilege. Hide your guilt. Well, Riggs, we'll drop it, but I've got other issues with my "friend" Peggy. Ever since her father's statue went up in Washington. It's *his* Lincoln this and *his* Lincoln that . . . isn't he supposed to be the country's Lincoln?
Lewis:	Miss Betty, let's focus on what the hospital can do for you.

Betty: Riggs, I asked you weeks ago to certify my sanity. Certify me so a Rabbi will believe me when I say I want to be a Jew.

Lewis: A Jew? . . . But why?

Betty: Again you ask why? Why? The white anglos might have the money now and they sit in the governors' and presidents' offices, all the while saying in church—The meek shall inherit the earth. Don't you believe a word they say about the meek. Letting a patient pretend he's KKK? You thought that was ok? Our days are numbered and I'm no Dumb Dora. Dust-to-dust my Anglican self. I'll only be un-numbered if I get out of here and become a Jew. The Jews know a lot more than any of us and . . .

Lewis: Do you know any? Personally, I mean. Is there someone you especially admire?

Betty: Now that, my good Dr. Riggs, is the most intelligent question you've asked me yet. Very interesting . . . let me consider it . . . hmmm . . . why yes, yes! It would be Emma Lazarus. Jew-ess and po-e-tess. Essence in the -*ess*. And she was as rich as any of them. Hah! "I lift my lamp beside the golden door!" Let's emphasize the gold! And I've always thought the Statue of Liberty's face

	resembled mine, and to think I might have my own words on a statue. What do you think, Riggs? Riggs, Riggs!
Lewis:	Go on. Tell me more.
Betty:	I'd even help Emma with her charity, The Society for the Improvement and Colonization of Eastern European Jews. Doesn't that sound like important work? To help all the poor immigrants. Now that would show Peggy. Her father's not the only sculptor in this country. I'll show her, indeed! Don't you agree, the Statue of Liberty is far, far more important than that Lincoln of hers in Washington?
Lewis:	Miss Betty, perhaps . . .
Betty:	After all, Lincoln was just a man. The man had his faults. If you knew history you'd know he was almost forced into freeing the slaves. And then he—Peggy's father that is—makes this monument of him. It's idol worship, if you ask me. Idol worship, the idylls of the idle rich. Idol-idyll-idle. Twing-twang-twum, I'll give them a taste of my thumb. But Lady Liberty, our "Mother of Exiles" . . . Oh Emma, Emma Lazarus, oh Lazarus, rising from the dead. Don't you Jews say Kaddish for the dead? Teach me how.

Lewis: Miss Betty, your words are so fast, they almost lift me up.

Betty: Fast words? Hah! You want them fast? Race you to the moon? I think it's a new moon tonight, sliver-thin. Don't you Jews say prayers to the new moon?

Lewis: Yes, and remember I'm Dr. Lewis. From New York.

Betty: *You* remember it! You don't think I know where I am? Or when I am? Maybe *you* don't remember who you are. Ok, Dr. Lewis from New York. Show me. Show me the money. Show me the goods. Show me the poems. You think the old poets of then can fix the new problems of now? All you Jews have some poet in you. You need a little help? Who are *your* friends? Perhaps I can help *you* recall . . . or let me call you . . .

Lewis: Call me what?

(the calling)

Call me Whitman
                    calling Lincoln
all across the country
calling Worcester calling Gloucester

across the state across the county
call to Pittsfield Call me Melville
call to Lenox Call me Hawthorne

Call to Owen and his war
        Call to Pound and his
        Call me fascist Call me traitor
        calling troops to surrender—

(Let it rain and snow on me—
        canto-ing in a Pisan cage—
when the raft broke and the waters went over me—
mind-crack, put away twelve years

in St. Elizabeths, DC Government Psychiatric)
Olson visits Call Saint Bishop . . .
        where are the women, the women?
Call MacLeish, lawyer/poet/public servant

a call to Cummington: *America Was Promises*
        call to court—a creative plea—*By Reason of*
        Insanity—humanity profanity Christianity—
A poet should not be mean, but be!

calling Frost calling Kunitz calling Ginsberg
doctors calling poets calling doctors calling poets
Call me Williams Call me Gilbert Call me
       doctor-poet

   calling   across the field
call me crazed in this need to write
call me
         and I beg the word

(at home that night, a dream announces itself with this title: "Overheard at the Asylum's Door"— he jots down the first scene; the second scene
perhaps occurring beyond the dream)

                    Scene 1.

Riggs: We have only a few more minutes today.
              Have you more to say?
              (Silence.) My dear Miss Betty . . .

Betty: My dear Dr. Riggs. It depends on who I am,
              or rather, who I will become.
              Do you yet know?

Riggs: (Sounding impatient.) Use *your* imagination,
              not mine.

Betty: Hmmm . . . "This is a world of books gone flat.
                    This is a Jew in a newspaper hat
                    that dances weeping down the
                    ward . . ."

              A lady poet, I am thinking . . .

Riggs: Stop it! (Riggs shows his mean streak.) Not
              that much imagination! The bee's knees! I said
              use *your* imagination! You're reciting a poem by
              Bishop not written for another twenty-eight
              years! And let me tell you, *your* recitation is
              about the wrong hospital! (Furniture shuffling.)

Betty: My good doctor, I am so sorry. Is my new
              self plagiarized? You're making me even more

guilty. Where oh where is Mammie-doll?

(Sobbing. Lewis knocks, goes in. On the threshold he faces Riggs, the Austen Riggs.)

Riggs: And just who might you be, young man? (Lewis shrugs as Riggs inspects his visitor's badge.) "Visiting psycho-analyst-poet." Looks legit. You legit? Hard day? Me, too. What troubles do you bring to our house of human troubles? I'm trying to tell my patient here, dreams don't tell the future. No, no, no! I'm not a Jungian. I'm certainly no Freudian. I'm just a humanist. And you . . .

Lewis: Me? If you want to listen I'll bring you all the world's troubles! Our own country's never been in worse shape. Almost a dictator at the helm. Race relations. Poverty. Worldwide refugees everywhere. Kids living hungry, separated from their mothers at the border. How would you feel watching your family shot or macheted or abducted? I'm going mad? There's Russia. More madness. Putin.

Riggs: (With a quizzical look.) Do you mean Rasputin? We dined just last week with a lesser Romanov cousin. Just five years since their revolution. I do think the czars will return. Don't you?

Lewis: Stop it! (Irate.) Stop! Have you any idea? The world is insane and you're acting insane, too. Aren't you supposed to be treating insanity here?

Riggs: (Voice mellowing to therapeutic.) There, there. It will be just a moment . . .

(Lewis see that Riggs reaches to push the emergency button which will call in the orderlies. Lewis rushes at him, hand-muzzles his mouth, pushes him to sit, declares . . .)

Lewis: Violence doesn't feel all that bad. Not at all. I should have tried it sooner!

Betty: Good for you, Lewis! The power of words! (She rolls up her sleeves.) And Riggs, don't you dare call for the wet packs on him!

(A knock.)

Lewis: The orderlies?

Betty: Block the door!

(The door opens. An elegant gentleman enters.)

Riggs: (Stammering.) Check his identification.

W.E.B.: No need, my friends. (His voice, a pure bell.) Dr. W. E. B. Du Bois, at your service . . .

Riggs: Doctor of what?

W.E.B.: Sociology. Isn't that what we all now need? We must study this society. We all do live here. You know, Dr. Lewis, the individual can struggle only so much, cannot go on in double lives. *Lift the veil*—to quote myself, or—*The train's in the station. Jim Crow won't keep you from sitting with us* . . .

Betty: A new doctor? A second opinion?

W.E.B.: If you wish, madame.

Betty: Dr. Riggs won't help me with my guilt. Can you? He makes it worse.

W.E.B.: As I have told, I am a sociologist. Your guilt is not of much concern to black folks.

Betty: Oh dear, oh dear. (She clutches Mammie abreast.) I sleep better with her.

(Du Bois takes the dollie, turns it over once. The dress falls revealing a White dolly, again a turn, the Black. Back, forth, back and forth. The Black becomes the White, the White the Black—all are mesmerized.)

W.E.B.: The topsy-turvey golliwog. If only it were that simple . . . if only . . .

(Du Bois offers Dollie back to her.)

Come take my hands.

(They each take one of its hands as if swinging a young child between. Dr. Lewis takes Du Bois's right hand, Betty's left. Riggs approaches, joins in, the circle slowly turning clockwise, then counter-, then clockwise again, as if they turned the spring of a great proclaiming clock. Dollie twisting between Black and White. All goes white, all goes black.)

All: (They continue circling with deliberate steps.)

We are the circle.

(Knocking again. A WWI-era vet enters. All look on, surprised.)

Vet: We're everywhere, but please, please. Rest in peace.

All: Join us. We are the circle.

Scene 2.

(he's missed . . .)

asylum words
impatient words

words wanting to
free words wanting to

free worlds
            he has crossed
a line
      letting a patient's

rush of syllables become his
crazed words becoming his

in the moment of joining her
and beyond, becoming the poet's

words—
      white coats opening like wings

(from the porch, I'm listening)

can listen.   Without echo
of the old   the new, the sound

O you singer solitary, singing
By yourself, projecting me,

Projecting myself without her,
singer-wife; how once I lent

my voice to hers, depleting
my breath while she sang on

the words of others   my voice
left unheard   unlived the life

unheard, its shreds returned,
came back, returning in

odd words inventing the new,
in phrases, I wrote a scatter

of notes in patient charts,
on newspaper margins, lists,

words coalescing into line,
lines from everyday talk;

praise first Dr. Williams,
doctor of the art of listening—

outside, outside myself—
doctor of the art of saying.

(further back in the field)

trees planted in the first year,
what might have been an orchard.

Peach-tree stumps, long felled,
and two leggy pears, barren

except for the year after
the Great Divorce. Heartache.

It was then this pair of trees
gave out bushels of fruit, saying

"Sweetness for your unpaired self,
one day, perhaps, another pair."

In an abandoned garden patch,
uncovered, a rusty scythe.

Holding it, I scratch a soil line
into this flowering field.

(at the wood-line, remembering)

No footprints, but in the air—sprung
from crushing steps—flow of thyme.

Along the far end of the property, a fence
almost lost in the grasses, by the last post

a letter that fell from my pocket, found
by the persistent Caretaker watching over,

left on the porch, put before me as if
he knew the contents, left many seasons

through rounds of rain and drizzle. The words
an oozing wound only half washed clean.

I, as husband, wrote it   years ago
when people still wrote letters, lovers

held the written words, the words of letters
breathed. The envelope unopened, addressed

to her, once-wife. Does the ink of the words
still hold to the page inside?   "Despite all,

I might still find a way back . . . " I might
have. Or . . .   The letter doesn't seem

to be mine, the Caretaker put it
before me again saying be reminded. Re-

mind the words   if words are refused,
so is memory   and the letter's ore

will open, an abandoned mine   I write a line
a letter to myself for myself   to words

and worlds be paired   she kept me
guessing her infidelity kept me following

her tracks, finding proof of the,
the unimaginable   inside that envelope

little breath is left   across the field   un-
imagined in the wind-flowers   in the wild

cosmos   everyday more proof   what I
find and trust   the other, shred for another nest

(Adam prepares a new flowerbed)

Even the common
garter snake has senses
so acute, a whiff
of deodorant spikes
its radar tongue.
The morning birds
give their best before
sun-dawn and human
rising into the pale air,
the unanswered.

Among the annuals,
amidst the perennials
knowing which plants
will grow and spread,
what needs replenishing,
a bank of daylilies,
(Spend their yellows!)
an orange tiger eye
staring into the sun
(jubilant and blinded).

(turning back to the porch)

Turning into Dwelling. Lord, am I ready?
My colleague, Dr. Gilbert, asking.
Poet, healer, how *the crickets' sonic party*
clicks deep in the grass outside, and I wonder
how many generations of these crickets
since he heard them in Worcester, these
sons and daughters of sons and daughters.
I join him, walk along in the *language house*
he builds out of anguish, beyond anguish,
my Black block that rose up in me like a grief—
for the poor blocks crumbling this country
now raising up this country. I follow his lead,
unmapped footsteps of this summer night come down.
In his dream, *poetry is need.* I say, and mine.
                      I say—amen.

(from *Look* Magazine, 1968, the painting)

The Right to Know protests the war in Vietnam. War
raging. A canvas of town faces facing out. A face-off.

In its center, the face of a young man, high-school age,
who grew up in The Dormouse, his late mother a friend
of the late Mrs. Rockwell. Among the town faces, his.
(My age, a biologist living in Glasgow, drives by to see
the house, tell some stories. I stand in the picture, too.)

The rage of a war no one wanted to fight. The canvas cannot
remain silent. Accompanying the painting, Rockwell writes:

. . . And listen to us, you who lead, for we are listening harder for the truth
that you have not always offered us. Your voice must be ours, and ours
speaks of cities that are not safe, and of wars we do not want, of poor
in a land of plenty, and of a world that will not take the shape our arms
would give it . . . We are the governed, remember, but we govern too.

And in this same year, 1968, Rockwell and King advocate
for the establishment of a Du Bois memorial home-site.

(The National Mall, Washington, D.C.)

On the Mall in front of the Monument
 where Daniel Chester French's Lincoln sits:

1922, Memorial Day, dedication of Monument,
 50,000.

1925, Ku Klux Klan,
 40,000.

1939, Marian Anderson, barred by the D.A.R.
 from the National Cathedral,
  50,000, and nationwide radio broadcast.

1945, Nazi genocide,
 400 rabbis.

1959, M.L.K., "Give us the ballot,"
 25,000.

1963, M.L.K., "I have a dream,"
 250,000.

1969, National Mobilization: End the War in Vietnam,
 600,000.

1978, Longest Walk, Native Americans trek
 3,000 miles from San Francisco across the country.

1989, March for Women's Rights,
500,000.

1993, LGB Rights and Liberty,
800,000.

1995, Million Man March,
837,000.

2004, March for Women's Lives,
1,100,000.

2010, March for America, immigration reform,
200,000.

2017, Women's March (Against Trump),
1,500,000.

(Lincoln's First Inaugural Address,
Monday, March 4, 1861)

We must not be enemies . . .

All over this broad land
will yet swell the chorus . . .

by the better angels of our nature.

(last Sunday afternoon broadcast of the season,
the Orchestra with the Berkshire Choral Society)

Not in the hands of boys, but in their eyes
Shall shine the holy glimmers of good-byes—
Owen's Great War, Britten's *Requiem*
together a monument to loss.

No mockeries now for them; no prayers
nor bells: on the front, lives exploding
in front of him, Owen takes them
into his words. How much shrapnel

can his stanzas hold? He never
becomes a vet, soul-marked
in injury's maiming aftershock.
Symphony cymbals crash rebuke,

sting Lewis's ears. A life lost is not
a life abridged, a second chance
scattering blooms of remembrance,
their flowers the tenderness of patient minds

against the dark sun, *the kind old sun—*
what bells ring, what timpani beats
the pulse of the forward-marching day.
Think how it wakes the seeds,

Woke, once, the clays of a cold star. . .
Was it for this the clay grew tall?

He sits with the text's ending,
from *Strange Meeting: I knew you
in this dark: for so you frowned.*
He had soldiered through a marriage,

strange meeting now with the soldier
of the requiem. *Let us sleep now.*
Let us say Kaddish, *Let them rest in peace. Amen.*

(imagining Adam's meditation)

   the long boat that arrives before living begins
that survives the flood.
                       (Not the boat that comes
after living, that moves into *the rolling fog*
and the *dear ones*, the ones being waved to,
have *already lost their faces*, the boat that absolves
the burdens of *all that caring*.)   This is the boat

that loves   the waters of earth and the earth
of earth, loves the gravel sound of beaching
under its hull   happy to tip to its side
astride the forest, to let its kept animals back
onto the earth   content to be taken apart
plank by plank, to be burned in a family hearth

or if pieces drift away they drift to drifting
across the blue seas, or the green, drift
to other uses   or to none, or if   it was
not a boat, it will be a train;   it will be
a kind of transport only approximated here,   it is
the coming before
                       before the going beyond.

(night)

the rise behind the sparkle-bush and viburnum—
        childhood's never-still-swing tips its to-and-fro-lilt
the earth continues its imperceptible spin I sit in the
        swing's lean sling and lean and pull into the night air my feet
climbing the dark road's stair pull up into and through the past
        thought distilled and harmonized companion-voices
instilled no more willed than a breeze-brimming echo

           my cup-hands goblet-fill with near-sky
                              I sip a full draft into breath

(last day, summer's end, waiting again at the
Crossing)

The blinking stops.
The bells stop.
   If bells of . . .
The thin arm silently
swings up, teetering.
It points to the sky.

The train's last echo
slows, and beyond
the field, sky, I, he
walks on, if into sky.
Closer to. Visions of.
Pulled up, lifted through.

Rise up and hear the bells
the unremembered,
unnamed, the far train's
engine out of the west
lows, a single *te-ki-ah*
bestowed, dark car behind

honking impatience—
Get on with you!—speeds
around, a spattering
of gravel-fall, progress.
Into the dusk-dim road.
The dust grows tall.

        Get on with you.

NOTES

p.4 In the early twentieth century, New York State began to construct asylums originally conceived as "farm colonies" for the insane. At its peak Pilgrim State, for instance, housed 13,875 chronically ill psychiatric patients and Creedmore, 7,000. While care was often negligent, if not abusive, the down-sizing or closing of these facilities was poorly planned and meant turning out many truly handicapped individuals to the streets. This was equally negligent, if not abusive in other ways.

p.7 Daniel Chester French (1850-1931), American sculptor, best known for the statue of Abraham Lincoln (1920) in the Lincoln Memorial in Washington, D.C.; Margaret French Cresson (1889-1973), French's daughter; Harriet Beecher Stowe (1811-1896), abolitionist and author of *Uncle Tom's Cabin*, the novel that brought the plight of African-American slaves to the attention of the white public; Lyman Beecher, Harriet's father (1775-1863), preacher who first encouraged debate on abolition, then recanted; Mrs. (Edith) Wharton (1862-1937), American novelist and full-time resident of the Berkshires from 1902-1911; her neice Beatrix Farrand (1872-1959), American landscape architect. The correspondence between Daniel Chester French and his daughter is maintained in the Chesterwood Archives, Williams College, Williamstown, Massachusetts. The plans for the renovation of The Dormouse can be found in the Library of Congress. The porch photo was taken at The Dormouse in early September, 1922. The Chesterwood Archives (Williams College) identify the woman on the left as Peggy Cresson and the man on the right as William

Penn Cresson; next to him Grace Lambert, and the woman next to Peggy as "unknown." A former neighbor, Frances Antonazzi, perhaps now deceased, worked in the French household many summers as a teenager serving meals. In a personal communication she insisted that the middle two women were Mrs. Hilda Beecher Stowe, on the left, and her sister next to her, Miss Gertrude Smith, not Mrs. Grace Lambert. The photo is attributed to Dr. Walter Lambert, New York physician.

p.10 The Taconic State Parkway is a 104.12-mile divided highway between Kensico Dam and Chatham, the longest parkway in the state of New York. It follows a generally northward route midway between the Hudson River and the Connecticut and Massachusetts state lines along the Taconic Mountains. Its hilly route was designed by landscape architect Gilmore Clarke to offer scenic vistas. Construction began in 1923. The town of Taghkanic, Lake Taghkanic, and Taghkanic Creek retain the spelling closer to the Native American meaning "in the trees," a name often used for a Lenape Chieftain.

Beauty and the Beast is a 1991 American animated musical romantic fantasy film produced by Walt Disney Feature Animation and released by Walt Disney Pictures. Lyrics by Howard Ashman and score by Alan Menken, winning the 1991 Academy Awards for Best Original Song and Best Original Score.

p.11 Loosely references a Lenape/Mohigan creation story.

p.13-14 The great physicians of Sephardic Spain, chief among them Maimonides (1135-1204), in Hebrew known as Mosche ben Maymom, in Arabic, Musa bin Maymun. Not only one of the greatest Torah scholars of all time, but one of the greatest physicians of his age. Equally at home in the Jewish and Arab worlds, he practiced with bi-cultural competence. Born a generation after Yehuda Halevi, one of the greatest poets of Medieval Sephardic Spain, Maimonides would have known his poetry but distrusted all poetry.

Stanley Kunitz (1905-2006), American poet from Worcester, Massachusetts. *Passing Through* (1995), his final collection of new poems. Quotes from *The Testing-Tree* (1971). Harvard's refusal to admit the future U.S. Poet Laureate for doctoral studies because he was a Jew was, of course, not unprecedented. Lionel Trilling writes in his doctoral dissertation on the Victorian writer Matthew Arnold how his father, "Thomas Arnold, a prominent educator and liberal church leader, opposed the admission of Jews to London University because it would mark 'the first time that education in England was avowedly unchristianized for the sake of accommodating Jews.'" Trilling himself was at first denied tenure at Columbia because, "as a Freudian, a Marxist, and a Jew you could not be happy as a tenured professor at Columbia." (source: Edward Alexander, "Mosaic" on-line 10-11-18) The ongoing denial to Israeli scholars in various functions at European universities as a political statement on middle eastern politics is not unrelated to the antecedent academic anti-semitism.

p.16 Clark University, located in Worcester, MA, sponsored in 1909 a series of lectures by Sigmund Freud, Carl Jung and other early psychoanalysts. Both were awarded honorary degrees by Clark. After initially seeing in Jung an heir-apparent, Freud dismisses and demeans him over disagreements of theory. Kunitz is influenced by Jung. The line "fathers kill sons and vice versa," refers to Freud's Oedipal theory which perhaps was in play banishing Jung from his inner circle. The quote is from Kunitz's "The Snakes of September" (1995). In the photo below, 1909, at Clark University, Freud (first row, left) and Jung (first row, right) flank Clark President C. Stanley Hall. Behind them, the devoted "followers," Brill, Jones, and Ferenzi. Note the cigar in Freud's hand. He was never without one.

p.16-17 William Penn Cresson (1873-1932), author, statesman, architect, husband of Peggy Cresson; Wilfred Owen (1893-1918), English poet who wrote from the trenches about World War I; a quote from his "Dulce et  Decorum Est" (1917). Also quoted from Walt Whitman's "The Wound-Dresser" (1896). The conversation references William Thayer (1897-1933), judge on the Superior Court of Massachusetts who presided over the Sacco and Vanzetti trials.

p.22 Patty Hearst (1954) granddaughter of American publisher William Randolph Hearst, was kidnapped and raped by an American terrorist group known as the Symbionese

Liberation Army. Found after nineteen months, she had become a fugitive wanted for serious crimes. At her trial, the prosecution claimed she joined the Symbionese Liberation Army of her own volition. She was found guilty of bank robbery. Hearst's sentence was commuted by President Jimmy Carter and she was later pardoned by President Bill Clinton. Quotes from the Manifesto of the S. L. A.

p.26-27 "This train" references Woody Guthrie's song, "This Train is bound for Glory." W.E.B. Du Bois (1868-1963), African-American sociologist, historian, and co-founder of the NAACP. Though Frederick Douglass first used the term "color line," Du Bois also used this phrase. His boyhood homesite is located off Route 23 in Great Barrington, MA. "And safely into a century of freedom," refers to the freedom suit filed in 1780 by Theodore Sedgwick from Stockbridge on behalf of Elizabeth "Mumbet" Freeman, effectively ending slavery in Massachusetts. She was a distant relative by marriage of Du Bois. (See note, p.47) "There in the fragrant pines…" from "When Lilacs Last in the Dooryard Bloom'd", Walt Whitman. "At Harvard, not of Harvard," attributed to Du Bois. "A temple of compromise….," from *The Crisis*, NAACP publication, May, 1922. The quote, "Will you please let us know…," is from a letter written to W.E.B. Du Bois by a Clark University history class. It was originally quoted in Michael Harper's poem "Deathwatch" (1970). The original design of the Lincoln Memorial by Clark Mills shortly after the assassination showed a Lincoln signing the Emancipation Proclamation. This version of the statue was blocked by conservative members of Congress, thus supporting Du Bois' view that French's statue honored the re-establishment of the Union, not emancipation. Still, the statue is filled with tension and conflict, not a monolithic representation of victory.

p.29 Gullah, also called Sea Island Creole English or Geechee, is a creole language spoken by the Gullah people, an African-American population living in coastal regions of the American states of South Carolina and Georgia. *The Souls of Black Folk,* W. E. B. Du Bois's seminal work, 1903. "Fa heal de tree, tek cyear de root," a Gullah expression meaning, to heal the tree take care of the root.

p.31-32 Arlo Guthrie's song monologue "Alice's Restaurant Massacree" takes place in Stockbridge and became an iconic song of protest against the War in Vietnam. In its full version it lasts nearly twenty minutes. The deconsecrated church where Guthrie lived is located near the train crossing identified as the Glendale Crossing. A further note, Norman Rockwell's first studio in Stockbridge was situated above Alice's Restaurant.

p.34 Ursula Andress (b. 1936), Swiss actress best known for her role as Honey Rider in the film *Dr. No* (1963). Sean Connery (b. 1930), Scottish actor best known for his James Bond roles.

A screen-shot from *Dr. No.*

p.37 While the doctor-poet and nurse-poet are identified as William Carlos Williams and Walt Whitman, in another poem the nurse-poet might have been Denise Levertov, a

World War II nurse. Her father was a Rabbi turned Anglican minister (how well he would have fit into this "transitioning" Glendale). Levertov came to the U.S. to meet William Carlos Williams, so it is imaginatively plausible they would have met in a surgical theater, operating on the budding poet's ear. (Interesting possibility, but not part of this story.)

p.37 The Dakota 38 refers to the 38 men of the Dakota nation hanged on Dec 26, 1862, after a speedy military "trial," in the aftermath of the U.S.-Dakota War of 1862. Initially, 303 were found guilty. Lincoln reviewed all the cases and pardoned 265. His not pardoning all 303 most probably was a means to avoid sabotage by his generals. *Coyote Medicine*, by Lewis Mehl-Madrona, M.D., on Native American healing. *Whereas*, by Layli Long Soldier, references the Dakota 38. "Cruel hands..." from "When Lilacs Last in the Dooryard Bloom'd," by Walt Whitman, 1865.

p.40 Tanglewood, summer home of the Boston Symphony in Lenox, Massachusetts, built on the Tappan family estate donated in 1937. *Sea Drift*, a large-scale musical work for chorus and orchestra by Frederick Delius (1862-1934) completed in 1904. The lyrics of this work, some quoted, are drawn from Walt Whitman's "Out of the Cradle Endlessly Rocking" (1860).

p.42 "We two, no more," quotes Whitman's "Out of the Cradle Endlessly Rocking."

p.44-45 Robert Frost (1874-1963), American poet, Consultant in Poetry to Library of Congress (poet laureate), 1958-1959; Congressional Gold Medal for Poetry, 1960.

Quotes from "Directive." Stanley Kunitz (see also note to p.16) was twice poet laureate, in 1974 (then Consultant in Poetry, Library of Congress) and again in 2000. Final quote from a Kunitz interview from the author's introduction to *Passing Through*.

p.46 Christopher Gilbert (1949-2007), poet and psychologist who received his PhD in psychology from Clark University in 1975 and also taught psychology there briefly. He cofounded and led, from 1977 to 1981 with Etheridge Knight, the Worcester Free People's Artists Workshop. Quote from "The Surviving" in the posthumous collection *Turning into Dwelling*.

p.50 Allen Ginsberg (1926-1997), American poet, foremost among the Beat poets. Quotes from "Pull My Daisy," written with Jack Kerouac and Neal Cassady, 1948, and from "Howl," 1956. He established an artist's commune in Cherry Valley, New York, close to Worcester, New York. As noted, Glendale, Massachusetts, is almost perfectly equidistant between the two Worcesters.

p.52-53 "Disease as an experience…," Mary Baker Eddy (1821-1910), from New England, one of the founders of the Christian Science movement, author of *Science and Health* (1875). Mr. Clay, a teacher of sorts, did allow himself to be consumed by a cancer while praying for cure. "To till and to tend," from Genesis 2:15. "A plot of land/a plot of history" refers to the history of Stockbridge Mohigan, or Mohinga. Originally, they lived peacefully with English colonists, and at the time of the founding of Stockbridge collectively owned 2,300 acres (*Berkshire Magazine*, Sept 2018, p.20). First assigning communal land to individual Mohigan, the colonists progressively took their land through lawsuits and other "legal" means. In 1783, the Stockbridge-Munsee Mohigans set out west, eventually settling on approximately 2,500 acres of reservation land in Wisconsin. See also "list of The Property Deeds" following Notes.

p.55 Nathaniel Hawthorne (1804-1864) writes *The House of the Seven Gables* and *Tanglewood Tales* in a cottage in Stockbridge. Quote from "Wayside, Introductory," *Tanglewood Tales,* 1853. William Carlos Williams, American poet and physician (1883-1963). Quote from *Paterson, Book I* (1946). Marriage statistics from the McKinely Irvin Family Law website.

p.58 No-see-ums, a type of miniscule gnat. They can truly be a nuisance.

p.60 Elizabeth "Mumbet" Freeman (1742-1829), born a slave in Columbia County, New York. Theodore Sedgwick's daughter Catherine Maria (1789-1867), a novelist, wrote an account of Mumbet's life in *Slavery in New England*, published in 1853. Portrait here by Susan Ann Livingston Ridley Sedgwick, 1811.

p.62 French's studio was designed by Henry Bacon and built soon after the sculptor aquired the property in 1896. The Warner family farmhouse was replaced by a grander house a few years later, also designed by Bacon.  The phrase, "if the public can keep it...." is a paraphrase of Benjamin Franklin's answer to the question what type of government the United States could have, "A republic, if the public can keep it." This phrase is particularly relevant today when government institutions seems to be  crumbling. The statue of Lincoln was completed in 1920. The picture here of French in his studio at Chesterwood, c.1922, shows French working on the bust of Ambrose Swasey.  "Andromeda," 1929-1931, remained unfinished at French's death in 1931. Most of French's best-known works were public commissions; however, he seems to have created this lyrical sculpture for himself. Was he thinking of his daughter, then married already eight years, but not pregnant

again after an earlier miscarriage? He saw art as public work. Personal expression was not his primary concern, yet in "Andromeda" he seems to express something more personal.

p.66 Norman Rockwell (1894-1978), American illustrator and painter who lived and worked in Stockbridge, Massachusetts. Often dismissed as just an "illustrator," his work can be seen in the traditions of representational art as depicting an era of American life with wit and charm. He later turns to political themes. *The Gossips, The Runaway, Game of Marbles, Tough Call, Home for Christmas*—various paintings by Rockwell depicting town life. *Lincoln for the Defense* depicts a young, lanky Lincoln.

The population of Stockbridge in 1960 was 2,161, and the circulation of *Look* Magazine at this time, 53 million. The reach of Rockwell's images was enormous. Ruby Nell Bridges Hall (b.1954) was the first African-American child to desegregate the all-white William Frantz Elementary School during the New Orleans school desegregation crisis in 1960. Above—*The Problem We All Live With*.

p.68 Definition of "decimate" from the Merriam-Webster dictionary. *Judenrein* refers to a city or area declared "Jew free" by the Nazis.

p.70 Quote from *When Breath Becomes Air* (2015), by Paul Kalinithi.

p.72 *"Just for his time,"* quoted from Genesis 6, refers to a concept that, contrary to the idea of a fixed and absolute Old Testament morality, moral concepts evolved and were bound by the individual's epoch. Today's notions of "political correctness" tend to be "Old Testament" in the popular sense of absolute. "Hairy-mouth," one of the many names used by some Native Americans to refer to Caucasians.

p.74-80 In 1913 in the town of Stockbridge, Dr. Austen Fox Riggs opened The Stockbridge Institute for the Study and Treatment of the Psychoneuroses. In 1919, the Institute incorporated as the Austen Riggs Foundation. Elm Court was built in 1885 for William Douglas Sloan and Emily Thorn Vanderbilt, with 106 rooms, the largest shingle style home in the U.S. It was designed by Peabody and Stearns with the gardens designed by Frederick Law Olmstead. Chestnut Lodge, in Rockville, Maryland, opened in 1910 as a sanatorium for the care of nervous and mental diseases. Also referenced is Emma Lazarus's (1849-1887) poem "The Colossus," placed on the Statue of Liberty in 1903. An American poet and privileged Sephardic Jew, she was also the founder of "The Society for the Improvement and Colonization of Eastern European Jews." The social stratification among the Jews mirrored society's broader stratifications. Will and Agnes Gould established Gould

Farm in 1913 as a healing community in the Berkshire hills of Massachusetts. They welcomed guests who were experiencing emotional and psychiatric vulnerabilities to join them, working on the farm and sharing the joys and challenges of daily life in a kind, healthy community. (Gould Farm website.) The photo (below) is labeled "Puritan House, Stockbridge—Peggy in large hat—1919." Puritan House was a residence of the early Austen Riggs Hospital (Chesterwood Archives, Williams College.)

p.82 American author Herman Melville (1819-1891), from 1850 on lived at Arrowhead Farm, Pittsfield, Massachusetts, author of the novel *Moby-Dick,* with its iconic opening sentence, "Call me Ishmael." This sentence is also the title of the American poet Charles Olson's (1910-1970) critical work on Melville. Olson was born in Worcester, MA. He was greatly influenced by American poet Ezra Pound (1885-1972) who was arrested for treason at the end of World War II. American poet and lawyer Archibald MacLeish (1892-1982), helped fashion Pound's insanity defense. *America Was Promises* was the title of his sixteenth book of poetry (1939). MacLeish settled in Cummington, Mass., near Pittsfield. Pound was committed to the custody of St. Elizabeths Hospital in Washington, D.C. from 1946-58. St. Elizabeths, the first federal psychiatric hospital, opened in 1855. "When the raft broke…," Ezra Pound, from Canto LXXX (one of the Pisan Cantos). Christopher

Gilbert, poet and psychologist, see note page 46. Elizabeth Bishop (1911-1979), American poet born in Worcester, Massachusetts.

p.84-88 "The lady poet" is Elizabeth Bishop; quoted poem, "Visits to St. Elizabeths" (1950). "Topsy-turvy," as a word, contains multiple references. "Topsy" references a character in Harriet Beecher Stowe's novel *Uncle Tom's Cabin* (1852). A golliwog, or dolliwog, is used as a reversing doll (as described), but also references a Black fictional character in Florence Kate Upton's *The Adventures of Two Dutch Dolls and a Golliwogg* (1865). The character was made into a doll and became associated with anti-Black caricatures. "Wog" in British usage is a person who is not white. The pictures of the golliwog here are two ends of 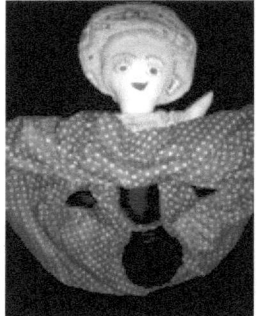  the same doll. Additional note on the golliwog: "The candy manufacturer Fazer is the largest producer of licorice in the country (Finland). In 1927, the company bought a British-Finnish biscuit-and-licorice company and released its signature line of sweet licorice the following year. The wrapper design featured a racist "golliwog" caricature, the British equivalent of a Sambo doll, which, depressingly, was not uncommon in itself — you can find historic examples of noxious candy packaging throughout the world — but which Fazer failed to jettison until 2007, in part under pressure from the European Union." (*New York Times* Sunday Magazine, *Salty Tooth,* October 28, 2018.)

p.90 Further quotes from Whitman's "Out of the Cradle Endlessly Rocking," and a fragment from Williams's "Sunday in the Park" from *Paterson* (Book 2).

p.96 Quotes from Christopher Gilbert's poem "Turning into Dwelling" from the book of the same name, and a fragment from his poem "Into the Into."

p.97 Rockwell's *The Right to Know* (*Look* Magazine, 1968) was intended as a critique of the Vietnam War. It was Rockwell's  last political work. William Earnshaw is the visitor, a biologist who lives in Glasgow, Scotland. Clemens Kalischer took a photo of him which Rockwell used in the painting. Earnshaw's face is first row, right of center.

p.98 The National Mall often refers to the entire area between the Lincoln Memorial on the west and east to the United States Congress, with the Washington Monument about midway. The area was first referred to as "The Mall" on an 1802 map.

p.101 Benjamin Britten (1913-1976), English composer of *The War Requiem* (1962), whose lyrics are extensively drawn from the poetry of Wilfred Owen, some quoted. Final lines from his "Strange Meeting." While *Kaddish* is a prayer recited at burials and at times to remember the dead, nowhere does it mention death. It is, in fact, a prayer affirming life.

p.103 Fragments quoted from "The Long Boat" by Stanley Kunitz.

p.104 The sparkleberry bush is a native species with white flowers in the spring, deep red leaves in the fall. The viburnum, also a native species, has larger white summer flowers and deep red fall berries. The name derives from Latin meaning "the wayfaring tree." Its red berries are a symbol in Russian culture representing a young girl's passion. It is also said to symbolically mean, "I die if neglected." The "goblet" references the ending of Frost's "Directive" and the holy grail.

p.105 "Rise up and hear the bells" from "O Captain! My Captain!" by Walt Whitman, 1865, his elegy to Abraham Lincoln, hero to Whitman and embodiment of the inclusive, democratic spirit. *Tekiah,* one of the calls of the shofar, the ram's horn blown to mark the beginning of a new year and spiritual renewal.

The Property Deeds:

1664, the Mohawk chase the Mahican from Albany. They flee to the lands that become Stockbridge. They hunt the woods of Glendale, fish the Housatonic. The Dormouse property is on land belonging to them.

1736, the Mohican "sell" a tract of land to the Warner's who productively farm it for several generations.

1781, the Mahican "deed" a tract of land to Isaac and Jonathan Ball that includes the Dormouse property.

1802, Marshall Warner, Isaac's son-in-law, purchases the property and builds a house, operates a boys' school and farms the land.

1815-1820, Warner constructs several "two over two" farm houses (two rooms upstairs and down) across the property.

1815, A Warner progenitor constructs several "two over two" farmhouses (two rooms upstairs and down) for offspring across the property.

1896, Marshall Warner sells 150 acres to Daniel Chester French.

1921, French deeds 10 acres to his daughter and her husband. In correspondence with her (letters in the Library of Congress), he designs the renovation of one of the old Warner farmhouses with multiple dormers; the "Dormer House" becomes "The Dormouse." It has always been painted gray.

1935, Peggy Cresson moves to Chesterwood after her father's death in 1931. She leases, then abandons, The Dormouse.

1961, Cresson sells a dilapidated house to the Earnshaws.

1973, The Earnshaws sell to Diana Potter, after her divorce. The Potters use the back ravine as a garbage dump.

1991, Potter sells to Dr. Lewis' family after the birth of his third child. He has the ravine filled in, creating a second field.

2011, Property fully deeded to Dr. Lewis after his divorce.

Index of Marriages (artists, writers, poets)

Bishop, E., 0
French, D. C., 1
Frost, R., 1 (plus a long-time companion)
Du Bois, W.E.B., 2
Gilbert C., 1
Ginsberg, A., 0
Hawthorne, N., 1
Kunitz, S., 2
Lewis, O., 2
MacLeish, A., 1
Melville, H., 1
Owens, W., 0 (killed in youth)
Pound, E., 1 (but…)
Rockwell, N., 3
Whitman, W., 0 (not the marrying type)
Williams, W., 1 (but…)

Acknowledgments

With gratitude—

To Fran Quinn, who read and reread, who cajoled and waited, made countless suggestions that helped shape this book through every revision;

To Martha Rhodes and Ed Hirsch, teachers and friends; and to Eugene McCarthy whose critical readings were decisive;

To my life-long friends Bob Abrams and Greg Egan who read almost monthly versions of the book as it progressed and kept rereading with unflagging interest;

To other friends and colleagues whose responses and support I deeply value: Paola Baccaglini, Judith Brisman, Wendy French, Carroll Joynes, Boris Thomas, Rita Charon, Kate Daniels, Jayne Benjulian, Richard Cohen, Arlene Stang, Donald Sanders, Cari Weil, Peter Dorward and Justin Hargett;

To my many students whose imaginations and eagerness to learn continues to inspire;

To Robert Murphy, publisher of Dos Madres Press, and Elizabeth Murphy, creators of beautiful books;

To Donna Hassler and Laurie Norton Moffatt, executive directors respectively at Chesterwood and the Norman Rockwell Museums, for their support and guidance with this project; Dana Pilsen, archivist at Chesterwood, for her research on Peggy Cresson's life, historic corrections to the manuscript, and assistance with permissions to reproduce photographs; to Margaret Rockwell and the Norman Rockwell Family Agency for permission to reproduce the Rockwell images.

And to my wife, Susan Ennis, whose love sustains my writing.

The poem on p.103 received the second prize in Scotland's 2018 Wigtown Poetry Award under the title *As if it didn't matter which way was home.*

Permissions to Reproduce Images:

The Clark University Archives, photograph in note for p.16.

The Chapin Library, Williams College, Gift of the National Trust for Historic Preservation / Chesterwood, a National Trust Historic Site, Stockbridge, Massachusetts, photographs on page ix and in notes for pp.7, 62 (interiors of studio), 74-80, and cover photograph.

Susan Ennis for photograph in note to p.62 and author photograph.

Massachusetts Historical Society, artwork in note for p.60.

Lucinda Miller for photograph of doll from her collection, note for p.84-88.

MGM Studios for reproduction of a film frame, note for p.34.

Norman Rockwell Family Agency and *The Norman Rockwell Museum* for reproductions of the artwork in notes for p.66 and p.97.

About the Author

OWEN LEWIS is the author of two prior collections of poetry, *Marriage Map* and *Sometimes Full of Daylight* (2017 and 2013 from Dos Madres Press), and two chapbooks. *best man* received the 2016 Jean Pendrick Chapbook Prize (The New England Poetry Club). Recent honors include 2018 Runner-up, Wigtown Poetry Competition (Scotland); 2017 Finalist, Pablo Neruda Award; 2016 Winner, International Hippocrates Prize for Poetry and Medicine. His poetry has appeared in *Nimrod*, *The Mississippi Review*, *Poetry Wales*, *Southward*, *The Four Way Review* and other journals. He is a professor of psychiatry at Columbia University in New York City where he teaches in the Department of Medical Humanities and Ethics.

OTHER BOOKS BY OWEN LEWIS
PUBLISHED BY DOS MADRES PRESS

SOMETIMES FULL OF DAYLIGHT (2013)
BEST MAN (2015)
MARRIAGE MAP (2017)

HE IS ALSO INCLUDED IN:
REALMS OF THE MOTHERS:
THE FIRST DECADE OF DOS MADRES PRESS - 2016

FOR THE FULL DOS MADRES PRESS CATALOG:
www.dosmadres.com

www.ingramcontent.com/pod-product-compliance
Lightning Source LLC
Chambersburg PA
CBHW030153100526
44592CB00009B/259